Only in Australia

Written by Mary Atkinson

Australia

My name is Scott. I live in Sydney, Australia. When I grow up, I want to work in an Australian wildlife park. Do you know the names of any Australian animals?

Contents

Look for the **Activity Zone!**
When you see this picture, you will find
an activity to try.

Meet the Platypus

Australia is a huge island in the southern half of the world. It is a country with forests, deserts, mountains, and plains. It is also home to a great number of interesting animals.

Many of Australia's animals have special features that make them different from other animals. One group is called the *monotremes*. They are mammals, but, like birds and lizards, they lay eggs.

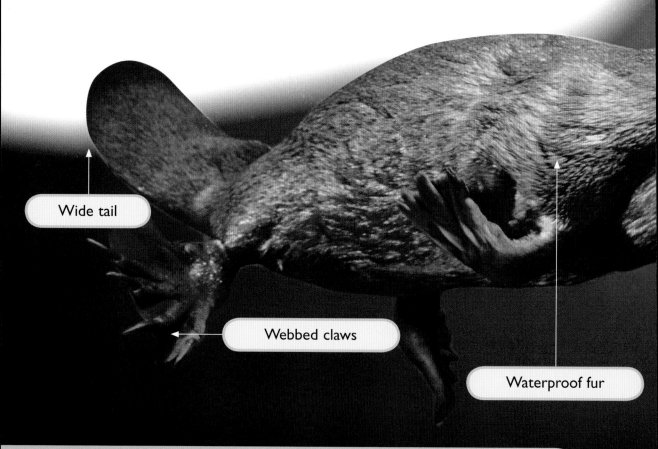

Wide tail

Webbed claws

Waterproof fur

mammals warm-blooded animals that feed their babies milk

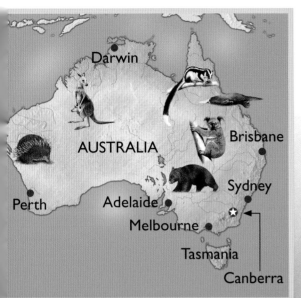

Large bill

There are only
two monotremes:
the platypus and
the echidna.

Egg-Laying Mammals

Female platypuses lay their eggs
in a burrow. They curl around
the eggs to keep them warm.

Echidnas have sharp spines and
a long snout. The females have a
pouch on their belly. They keep
their eggs warm inside the pouch.

Amazing Marsupials

Kangaroos, wombats, and koalas are marsupials.
Marsupials are a special type of mammal.
Their babies grow up inside a pouch on
their mother's belly.

There are marsupials all over Australia.
Some dig burrows, and others climb trees.
Some are as small as a mouse, and others
are as big as a grown man.

Koalas are often called *koala
bears*, but they are not bears
at all. They are marsupials.

When a joey is big enough, it pokes its head out of its mother's pouch.

A male kangaroo is called a *boomer*, a female is called a *flyer*, and a baby is called a *joey*.

All Sorts of Marsupials

There are nearly 300 different kinds of marsupials. Here are just a few.

Tree kangaroo

Quoll

Wallaby

Squirrel glider

Tasmanian devil

Virginia opossum

Not all marsupials live in Australia. Some **species** of marsupials live in New Guinea, and the opossums in America are marsupials, too.

species   a group of similar animals that can have babies

7

A Cozy Carriage

Newborn marsupials are very small. They have no fur. The first thing they do is crawl into their mother's pouch. There they drink milk, rest, and grow. When the mother looks for food or a new den, the babies go with her. They are warm and safe inside her pouch.

In time, the babies outgrow the pouch. However, their mother continues to look after them for a while longer.

A baby wombat leaves its mother's pouch after seven months.

When it outgrows the pouch, a baby koala travels on its mother's back.

Home Sweet Pouch

Newborn possums crawl into their mother's pouch. They are so small that they look like pink beans.

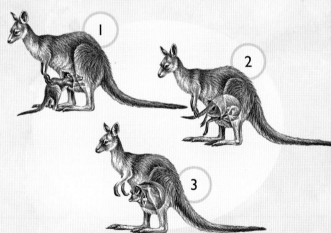

After a joey has left its mother's pouch, it often hops back in. It goes back to rest and to escape danger. It also rides in the pouch on long journeys.

Leaping and Gliding

Marsupials move around in many different ways. Most kangaroos cannot walk; instead they hop everywhere. Their huge hind legs are strong and can leap long distances—or give a powerful kick.

Gliders have flaps of skin joining their front and back legs. As they glide through the air from tree to tree, their flaps act like parachutes. Many tree-climbing marsupials have long tails, which they wrap around branches as they climb.

Front foot

Flap of skin used as a parachute

Gliders use their tails to change direction while they are in the air.

Tail

hind legs an animal's back, or rear, legs

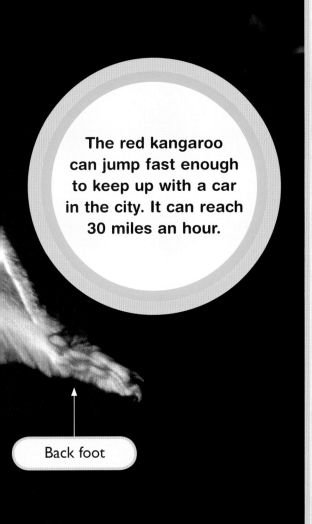

Possums use their tails to help them keep their balance when climbing.

The red kangaroo can jump fast enough to keep up with a car in the city. It can reach 30 miles an hour.

Back foot

Paws and Claws

An animal's feet suit its lifestyle. Marsupials that live in trees have a toe on each back foot that acts like a thumb. It helps them hold on to branches as they climb.

Wombats have wide feet with strong claws. These feet help them dig.

Webbing in water   Webbing on land

The platypus has webbed front feet for swimming. On land, it pulls back the webbing so it can walk and dig easily.

Face Facts

Many marsupials are nocturnal. They have big eyes to help them see in the dark. Marsupials that glide or jump from branch to branch often have eyes that face forward. This helps them see exactly where to land.

Many small Australian animals have long noses, which help them sniff out insects, grubs, and worms to eat. Plant-eating marsupials, such as kangaroos and koalas, have short noses.

nocturnal active at night, not during the day

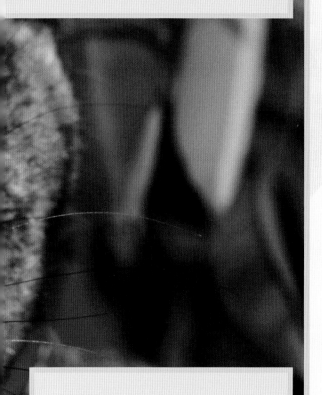

The bandicoot uses its long nose to feed on insects under the ground.

Possums have big, forward-facing eyes. These help them see as they race along branches in the dark.

Made for Swimming

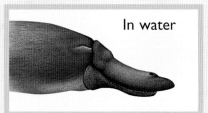

In water

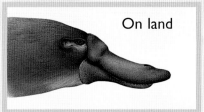

On land

Platypuses cover their eyes and ears with a flap of skin when they dive.

Underwater, the platypus's bill sends out electric signals, like radar. The signals help it find and catch small creatures.

Keeping Cool

The middle of Australia is a hot, dry desert. The animals that live there have special ways of keeping cool and of staying alive without much water.

Bilbies are small marsupials that live in the desert. They dig long, deep burrows to sleep in during the day. At night, when it is cooler, they come out to find food. Their big ears lose a lot of heat, which helps cool them down.

Bilbies are endangered animals. Cats and foxes hunt them, and rabbits and cattle eat the same plants they do.

endangered an animal that could die out because so few are left

Marsupial moles use their huge front claws like flippers to "swim" through desert sand as they hunt for prey. Their claws also make good eating tools.

prey an animal that is hunted and eaten by another animal

What Are Numbats?

Numbats are endangered marsupials. They have striped brown coats that make them hard to see in the desert. At night, they seek shelter in hollow logs or in tunnels, called *burrows*. During the day they use their powerful claws to dig out and eat termites in their nests.

The numbat is one of the few animals in the world that has a name beginning with the letter *n*.

Spines, Spots, and Stripes

Many Australian animals have spines, spots, or stripes. These features have a purpose. Sharp spines hurt any predators that try to attack.

An animal's colors help it hide. Many animals are the same colors as their surroundings. Stripes and spots break up their shape, making them hard to see. This is called *camouflage*. It helps animals hide from predators or sneak up on prey.

The frogmouth is a very hard bird to spot. It hunts at night. During the day, it looks just like the branches on which it rests.

predator   an animal that hunts other animals for food

The echidna's spines protect it from predators. When another animal attacks, it digs into the ground so that only its spines show.

The striped possum has black and white stripes that warn away predators. It also gives off a horrible smell, just like a skunk.

Try this camouflage activity.

1. Pick four colors. Now imagine a planet far away. Using only your four colors, draw some land, plants, and sky on your planet. Fill in all the white space.

2. On another piece of paper, draw the outlines of three space marsupials. They can be as wacky as you like.

3. Color in the creatures using your four colors. Make one striped, one spotted, and one a solid color.

4. Cut out the animals and put them on the planet. Which is the easiest to see? Which is the hardest?

Desert Reptiles

Australia is home to many unusual reptiles.
Reptiles are cold-blooded animals, such as
lizards, snakes, and crocodiles. They need
to move in and out of the sun to keep their
bodies at an even temperature. This makes
them well-suited to desert living. Many
Australian reptiles have special ways
of protecting themselves.

temperature   how hot or cold something is

The Australian frilled lizard scares off predators by opening its mouth, hissing, and fanning out the frill around its neck.

A Day in the Life of a Lizard

1. At midday it shelters in shade.
2. It hunts for food in the afternoon sun.
3. In the late afternoon, it basks in the sun and digests its food.
4. In the cool of the evening, it finds a safe place to sleep.
5. It curls up in a ball to keep warm overnight.
6. At dawn, it wakes up.
7. It basks in the early-morning sun to get energy for the day.
8. By mid-morning, it is time once again to hunt for food.

The thorny devil lizard has spikes that scare off attackers. It also protects itself through camouflage.

Powerful Poisons

Australia is home to some of the most poisonous creatures in the world. The Australian small-scaled snake is the deadliest snake on Earth. Its venom is so strong that a single drop could kill 217,000 mice.

The Sydney funnel-web spider is probably the most poisonous spider in the world. It lives near people in city gardens; however, an anti-venom now saves many lives.

venom   a poison produced by an animal
         to capture or kill prey

Male platypuses have a poisonous claw on each hind leg. The venom is strong enough to kill a small dog.

Many snakes are hard to see because they are camouflaged to match their surroundings.

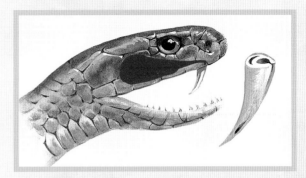

Small-scaled snakes have long, hollow fangs at the front of their mouth. Venom is injected through the fangs into the victim's body.

The funnel-web spider raises its head and then stabs its fangs down into its prey.

Staying Alive

In the 1800s and 1900s, many people moved to Australia. They built new farms, roads, and towns. As a result, the places where many native species lived became smaller and smaller. Settlers brought animals, such as cattle, dogs, and rabbits, into the same places. Many native animals were hunted, and some are now extinct. Others are endangered, but many people are working to save them.

extinct   when a plant or animal no longer exists because it has died out

Turning unknown land into farms was hard work. People thought Australia was so big that there would always be plenty of wild animals. They shot them for their fur and to clear land for farm animals.

Settlers took some brush-tailed possums from Australia to New Zealand. Now there are millions there. They have taken over the homes of many native animals. They are pests in New Zealand but not in Australia.

Visitors can see Australian animals up close at Healesville Sanctuary near Melbourne, Australia. The zookeepers take care of homeless or hurt animals. They also give talks to families and school groups.

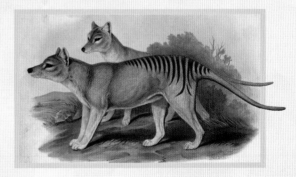

Tasmanian tigers were large, wolf-like marsupials. They ate sheep, so farmers started shooting them. The last Tasmanian tiger died in a zoo in 1936.

23

Find Out More!

1   Are there any animals that live mainly in your country? How are they suited to where they live?

2   Imagine that there were a snowy-mountain marsupial. What features do you think it would have?

To find out more about the ideas in *Only in Australia*, visit **www.researchit.org** on the web.

Index